SO-AZW-523

HOPSCOTCH
AROUND THE WORLD

Mary D. Lankford ILLUSTRATED BY Karen Milone

MORROW JUNIOR BOOKS   New York

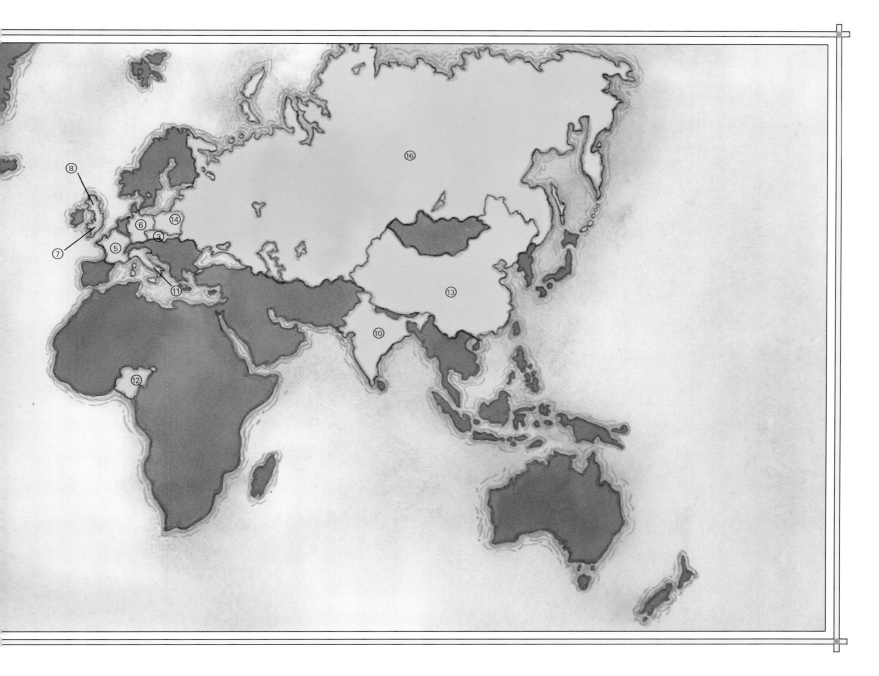

For my grandchildren, who hopped into my heart—
Christopher Shockley, Ben Houk, Jared Houk,
Jacob Lankford, and Caitlyn Roxanne Lankford

—M.D.L.

To Julia M. and John James K.,
two natural hoppers

—K.M.

ACKNOWLEDGMENTS

Children, older adults, teachers, and librarians contributed to this book by telling me about the hopscotch games they played as children. I appreciate the assistance I received from the following people in identifying and describing different versions of hopscotch: Ziomara Bonilla and Liliana Rico Arias for Peregrina and La Rayuela; Mollie Bynum, Maggie Ivanoff, Roz Goodman, Lucy L. Lau, Delma L. Apassingok, Trudy K. Apatiki, and Abraham Anasogak for Alaskan Hopscotch; Lynnette Jordan, Choy Man See Lau, and Rosemary Fraser for Jumby; Maureen Salinas for English versions of hopscotch; Epie Koster for Pele; Lucho Salinas-Estensorro for La Thunkuña and Pele; Mary Frank for Paradies Hüpfen; Millie Lee for versions of hopscotch played in San Francisco's Chinatown; Suk Lee for additional assistance; Ron Jobe and Beverly Braun for help in locating *Hopscotch* by Patricia Evans; and Teresa Moogan for her work in New York City collecting material from S. Z. Tresser (Klassa), Chana Klein (Kritz), Bill Miles (Ta Galagala), Lorraine Casey Moogan (Potsy), Gusta Rabinovich (Klassiki), and Geetha Rajendran (Chilly).

Design by Trish Parcell Watts
Printed in Hong Kong by South China Printing Company (1988) Ltd.
5 6 7 8 9 10

Library of Congress Cataloging-in-Publication Data
Lankford, Mary D.
   Hopscotch around the world / Mary D. Lankford ; illustrated by Karen Milone.
     p. cm.
   Summary: Presents directions for playing variations of hopscotch, an ancient game still played worldwide.
   ISBN 0-688-08419-2.—ISBN 0-688-08420-6 (lib. bdg.)
   1. Hopscotch—Juvenile literature. [1. Hopscotch. 2. Games.]
I. Milone-Dugan, Karen, ill. II. Title.
GV1218.H6L36 1992
796.2—dc20   91-17152   CIP   AC

Contents

Playing Hopscotch

Many people looked surprised when I told them I was writing a book about hopscotch. They wanted to know why. I usually responded by saying that one short sentence I read in a book aroused my curiosity. It referred to a hopscotch pattern found in an ancient Roman forum. I had always assumed that hopscotch was a special beloved game dating back only to my own childhood. I had also assumed, erroneously, that there was only one "right" way to play the game.

In truth, hopscotch has been played throughout history in almost every country of the world. Its few rules make it easy to learn. The pattern, chalked on a sidewalk or traced in dirt, may differ from place to place, but the basic idea is the same: Toss an object into the pattern and then hop into, through, and out of the pattern without touching the lines with either your feet or your hands. The object tossed is called by many names: *stone*, *lagger*, *potsy*, or *puck*, to name a few. The spaces between the lines are also called by many names: *squares*, *boxes*, *dens*, *beds*, *steps*, and *nests*.

The derivation of the word *hopscotch* has been debated by historians. Some believe *scotch* refers to the stone or other small item used as a puck. Others say *scotch* means a mark, or line, in this case on the ground—making *hopscotch* a game in which players "hop over lines."

Hopscotch is played by both girls and boys. Roman soldiers are believed to have brought it to Britain. One of the oldest known hopscotch patterns is still visible where it was inscribed on the floor of a Roman forum. Roman soldiers may also have drawn hopscotch patterns on the roads they were building in order to show British children a game from their own childhoods.

My search for different versions of hopscotch started in my own school library. Then I started using the public library and borrowing books through interlibrary loan from institutions all over the United States. Finally, I began to interview children and my contemporaries, asking them to describe versions of hopscotch they knew. My search finally broadened to include foreign embassies and friends of friends who were currently living abroad. Writing the book was a little like solving a mystery or putting all the pieces of a puzzle together. I doubt if I will ever stop asking people how they played hopscotch as children or stop looking for the word *hopscotch* in the index when I come across a book of games.

Like folktales, games take many forms. I am sure that there are many hopscotch variations not included in this collection. But no matter what pattern children draw or what they use for a puck, they are playing a game that is older than their school and their parents and older than the sidewalks and playgrounds on which the pattern is drawn.

Aruba

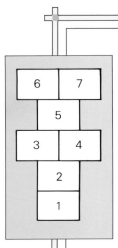

Pele   The island of Aruba in the Netherlands Antilles is just twenty miles north of the coast of Venezuela. Many of the trees on the island have been bent into unusual shapes by the strong winds that blow across the island. Because of these winds, an object that will not blow or roll away must be used as a puck. A stone or coin makes a good puck for the children of Aruba.

DIRECTIONS:

1. Throw the puck into box 1.

2. Hop into box 2. Then jump into boxes 3 and 4, putting one foot in each box.

3. Hop into box 5, and jump in boxes 6 and 7 just as you did for boxes 3 and 4.

4. Jump and turn, landing again in boxes 6 and 7, now facing the rest of the pattern.

5. Hop into box 5. Then jump into boxes 3 and 4, putting one foot in each box.

6. Hop into box 2, and pick up the puck from box 1. Hop out of the pattern without landing in box 1.

7. Throw the puck into box 2, and repeat the entire pattern. If the puck lands in the wrong box, or outside the pattern, you lose your turn.

8. Throw the puck into box 3. Hop into boxes 1 and 2 and then into box 4. Continue through the pattern and, on the way back, pick up the puck from box 3 while balancing on one foot in box 4. Never hop into a box with a puck in it.

9. If you step on a line, you also lose your turn, but your puck stays in place until you try again. Players cannot hop or jump into a box that holds either their own puck or that of another player.

10. The first player who completes the entire pattern wins the game.

Bolivia

The diagram shows a hopscotch pattern with the following spaces from top to bottom: el mundo, el cielo, domingo, viernes / sábado (with jueves below), miércoles, martes, lunes, baseline.

La Thunkuña

Bolivia, a South American republic snuggled between Peru, Brazil, Chile, and Argentina, names both La Paz and Sucre as its capital. Just as it has two capitals, it has two versions of hopscotch—an Old World version and a newer, contemporary one. The play of the game is identical in the old and new versions, and the shapes of the patterns are similar. But in the newer version, the spaces, except for *el mundo*, are numbered rather than named. Children today still use a stone for a puck, as their parents did, but they have also found that an orange or tangerine peel makes a very effective puck because it will not roll when tossed into the pattern. Really creative children may turn the peel into something that looks like a daisy chain.

DIRECTIONS:

1. Throw the puck into *lunes* (Monday). Hop over that space into *martes* (Tuesday).

2. Using your hopping foot, kick the puck out of *lunes* and back behind the baseline. Then hop out of the pattern. (Players can agree to stand on their hopping foot and kick with the other.)

3. Toss the puck into *martes*. Hop into *lunes*, then into *miércoles* (Wednesday). Kick the puck out of the pattern, and then hop out.

4. Repeat for *miércoles*, then for *jueves* (Thursday). When you throw the puck into *jueves*, hop into *miércoles*, and then jump into *viernes* (Friday) and *sábado* (Saturday), with one foot in each. Then hop on one foot into *domingo* (Sunday), and kick the puck back behind the baseline as before.

5. Do not throw the puck into *viernes* or *sábado*. Continue the pattern, throwing the puck into *domingo*, and then *el cielo* (heaven). Jump into *el mundo* (world) with both feet. Turn with a leap and then kick the puck past the baseline with your hopping foot as before.

6. Always hop over the space where the puck lands. If your puck lands on the wrong space on any toss or kick, you lose your turn. When it's your turn again, start where your last turn ended. The player who gets through the entire pattern first wins the game.

Czechoslovakia

beklo	raj
9	10
7	8
5	6
3	4
1	2

Kritz   Girls in Czechoslovakia were playing hopscotch, which they called Kritz, many years before World War II. *Kritz*, which means "to make a mark," is a kind of made-up word. Mothers sometimes use this word when they scold: "Don't you *kritz* on the walls!" The girls, and sometimes boys, draw their patterns on cement with a piece of chalk or coal. A piece of broken china or glass serves as a puck. There are ten boxes in Kritz, so it can take a long time to play. Even if you hop perfectly through all ten boxes, you still have to throw the puck into *raj* (paradise). If your puck lands in *beklo* (hell), you are out.

DIRECTIONS:
1. Toss your puck into box 1.
2. Hop into box 1. Pick up your puck. Hop out of the pattern.
3. Toss your puck into box 2.
4. Hop into box 1, then into box 2. Pick up your puck. Hop back into box 1 and then out of the pattern.
5. Toss your puck into each box in turn. Hop only as far as the box where the puck is; then pick up your puck, turn, and hop out.
6. When you have hopped through all ten boxes, try to throw your puck into *raj*. Be sure not to let it land in *beklo* or you'll have to go back to the beginning!
7. The first player to hop through boxes 1 through 10 without making a mistake and to throw the puck into *raj* wins.

El Salvador

el mundo

ala | ala

ala | ala

Peregrina *Peregrina* means "female pilgrim." Girls growing up in the countryside of El Salvador wear skirts, rarely shorts or jeans, and kick off their sandals when they play with their friends under the shade of mango trees. This fruit is knocked down from the trees with rocks. When the sweet mangoes are eaten, their large seeds can be used as pucks (called *tistos*). The *tisto* can also be a piece of rock or part of a roof tile. The game pattern is sketched in the dirt. There are few paved *calles* (streets), *callejones* (small streets or alleys), or sidewalks in the rural areas. Even if there were sidewalks, no one has chalk to draw the pattern. Chalk is available only in school classrooms.

DIRECTIONS:

1. Toss the *tisto* into the first box.

2. Hop over the first and into the second box.

3. You must not put your hands on the ground or step on any of the lines. If you do, your turn ends.

4. Stop and pick up the *tisto* while you are still standing on one foot in the second box. Hop over the first box and out of the pattern.

5. Continue to follow this pattern until you have successfully thrown the *tisto* into each box, picked it up, and then hopped back to the beginning. The *alas*, or "wings," are treated like the double boxes in Pele. Throw the puck first into the left *ala* and then into the right. Never jump into an *ala* with a *tisto* in it.

6. When you throw the *tisto* into the box below *el mundo* (world), jump into *el mundo* with both feet and then jump again, turning around as you do so. Pick up the *tisto* and start hopping back through the pattern and then out.

7. When you have completed the entire pattern, you can place an X or *bimba* (big stomach) in the first box. No other player can land in a square with your *bimba*.

8. No player can place a *bimba* in a square that has already been marked. If the first two squares have an X on them, the third player has to make a big jump to get over them. Luckily, the *alas* can be used to jump in on two feet.

9. The player with the greatest number of *bimbas* wins.

France

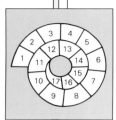

Escargot Snails are a favorite food in France. The spiral shape of the shell of a snail (*escargot* in French) is the pattern used for one variation of hopscotch played there. Escargot is one of the few hopscotch games in which no puck is used. The game is also called La Marelle Ronde (round hopscotch).

DIRECTIONS:

1. Before you begin hopping, decide which foot you will hop on. If you decide on your left foot, you must hop in and out each time on that foot.

2. Hop through the snail.

3. Hop only once in each space. No player may touch a line when hopping.

4. In the center space, you may rest on both feet.

5. After resting, turn and hop back to the beginning. Repeat the pattern once more.

6. After you have hopped in and out twice, choose one space for your "house." Write your initials in this space. This becomes another rest space for you. No other player may hop into your house.

7. The game ends when it is impossible for anyone to hop into the center space or when all of the squares have initials in them. The player who "owns" the greatest number of squares wins.

Germany

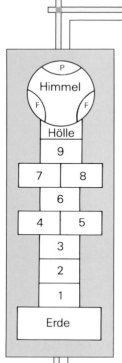

Paradies Hüpfen

Young people in Germany jump through the pattern of this game (which is also known as Himmel und Hölle) attempting to move from *Erde* (earth) through *Hölle* (hell) to *Himmel* (heaven). A flat rock, a piece of glass, or a cork from a wine bottle is used as a puck. The game is played so that you do not hop into the spaces marked with an F (for *Fegefeuer*, or purgatory) or into *Hölle*. The pattern is so divided because many people believed that heaven was divided—and paradise (P on the gameboard) was the inner sanctum of heaven.

DIRECTIONS:

1. Before beginning, players decide which of four tricks will end the game.

2. Stand in *Erde*. Toss the puck into box 1.

3. Hop on one foot from *Erde* into box 1, pick up the puck, and hop back to *Erde*.

4. Toss the puck into box 2, hop from *Erde* into box 1, then box 2, pick up the puck and toss it back into *Erde*. Then hop back to *Erde* yourself. Continue following this pattern until you get to box 9. (Rules for Pele and Peregrina apply to boxes 4 and 5 and boxes 7 and 8.) Your turn is over if your puck lands in the wrong space or if it lands on a line. You can begin where you made your mistake when your turn comes again.

5. After hopping from box 1 to box 9, throw the puck into *Himmel*. If it lands in an F space, you may skip doing the trick.

6. If the puck lands in *Himmel*, hop through the pattern to pick up the puck and return to *Erde*. Then toss the puck into box 9. Follow the pattern in reverse, tossing the puck into boxes 8, 7, 6, and so on back to *Erde*, hopping through the pattern each time.

7. If your puck lands in Paradise (P), you may not speak or laugh for the rest of the game.

8. If your puck lands in *Hölle*, your turn ends. Start from the beginning when it is your turn again. When you complete the pattern, you must complete the trick to win.

TRICKS:

a. Move the puck with your foot from box to box as you hop from *Himmel* back to *Erde*.

b. Balance the puck on one foot and hop through all the boxes. If the puck falls, your turn ends.

c. Balance the puck on your head as you hop through all the boxes.

d. Balance the puck on your knee.

19

Great Britain

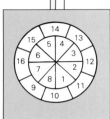

Hop-Round

An atlas will show you that England is part of a group of islands off the northern coast of Europe. Long before England became part of Great Britain, the area was invaded by Roman soldiers. The soldiers probably brought this game with them; the wheels on their carts looked just like the pattern they used for their board. Similar patterns have been found in the floor of a Roman forum. Each player uses five small pebbles.

DIRECTIONS:

1. Before the game begins, players should agree on what score will win the game.

2. Throw the pebbles, either one at a time or all at once, into the pattern. Add up the numbers assigned to the spaces into which the pebbles have fallen. This will become your score if you successfully hop into and out of the pattern.

3. When a pebble falls on a line, it doesn't count. Hop on one foot around the pattern until you reach a box with a pebble. Pick up the pebble, and hop to the next box with a pebble. You must do this without stepping on a line or placing your other foot on the ground.

4. If you pick up all five of your pebbles successfully, you may "claim" any section of the outer ("tire") part of the wheel or any of the inner sections between the "spokes."

5. The next player must hop over your "claimed" sector when picking up his or her stones.

6. The winner is the first player to reach the score the players agreed on.

Great Britain

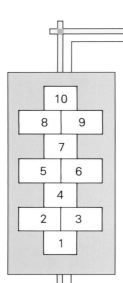

Scotch-Hoppers

Many of the school yards in England and Scotland are paved. It is on this paved area, or on sidewalks, that children play another version of hopscotch called Scotch-Hoppers, or Hop-the-Beds. Squares, or *beds*, are drawn with chalk or with a rock that makes a white mark. Small pieces of slate are used as pucks. Many home and school roofs are made of slate, and small pieces of this blue-gray rock make ideal pucks because they do not roll and are easy to throw. The pattern is washed away after playing the game.

DIRECTIONS:

1. Stand outside bed 1 and throw the puck into it.

2. Hop through the pattern and back to bed 1, pick up the puck, and hop out again. The only time you may put both feet down at the same time is in the double beds: 2 and 3, 5 and 6, 8 and 9.

3. On your second turn (after all players have completed their first turns), toss your puck into bed 2. Hop into each bed and back. As always, when you throw the puck into one of the double beds, do not hop into that space. Pick up your puck as you hop back out of the pattern.

4. If you miss the bed when tossing, you must start again from the beginning.

5. The first player to toss the puck and hop successfully into and out of all the beds wins.

Honduras

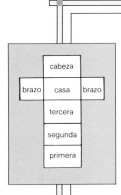

La Rayuela

Standing on the north or east coast of Honduras, you will see waters that are a mixture of both the Gulf of Mexico and the Caribbean Sea. Honduras is a part of Central America. Its countryside is so rugged that some areas are still unexplored. In Honduras, the game of hopscotch is called La Rayuela. The Spanish word *rayuela* means "line." The lines, or *rayas*, outline the pattern for this version of hopscotch, which is played by the Honduran descendants of Mayan Indians and *mestizos* (people of mixed Spanish and Indian blood). The word for the puck, *tejo*, comes from the Spanish word *teja*, meaning "tile." Children can pick up adobe roof tiles on the ground near many of the buildings. The pattern is traced in the dirt with a stick. The game is played by children in both urban and rural areas.

DIRECTIONS:

1. Stand outside the pattern and throw the puck into *primera*, the "first" box of the pattern. Hop through the pattern in the direction of the arrows. You may jump into the *casa* square, or "home," with both feet. Do not step on a line. If you do, you are out of the game. Retrieve the puck on your way out.

2. On your next turn, toss the puck into *segunda*, the "second" square.

3. Continue to hop from box to box.

4. After the "third" box, *tercera*, the next square you toss the puck into is *casa*. The puck is not tossed into *brazo* (arm) or *cabeza* (head).

5. If you fail to toss the puck into the right square, you are out of the game. The first player to complete the entire pattern without any mistakes wins.

25

India

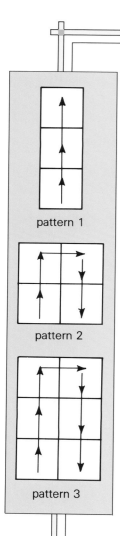

pattern 1

pattern 2

pattern 3

Chilly It is easy to use a stick to draw a hopscotch pattern in the soft red-clay earth of Pondicherry, a territory in southern India. If you are the one drawing the pattern, the smaller children will probably try to get you to make the boxes small so they can jump over them easily, while the bigger children, who can jump farther, may try to get you to draw bigger boxes so that they will win.

The meaning of the word "Chilly" seems to have been lost. Each player finds a flat, smooth stone to use as a puck, one that will be good for both tossing and kicking. The game starts with all the children wearing sandals, but before the end of the game, all will have kicked off their sandals. Both winners and losers will go home with the soles of their feet bright red from the clay.

There are a few different patterns. Some are more difficult than others. You do not draw any numbers in the boxes. The rules for all the patterns begin in the same way.

DIRECTIONS:
1. Throw your puck into the left-hand box closest to you (the first box in pattern 1).
2. Hop into the box with the puck in it.
3. Use your hopping foot to kick the puck into the next box. Continue until you are out of the pattern. (The arrows on the patterns indicate the direction to proceed as you hop and kick. If the puck lands on a line, you lose your turn.)
4. Pick up your puck and return to the base-line. Toss the puck into the box just above the first one.
5. Hop over the first box and into the second box. Kick the puck into the next box and continue to play as described above.

PATTERN 1:
6. Toss your puck into the top box.
7. Hop over the first two boxes and kick the stone out of the pattern.
8. Pick up your puck and walk around the

pattern to the first box. Turn your back to the pattern and toss the puck over your shoulder. Then face toward and jump into the box where the puck lands. Continue to play as described above.

PATTERN 2:

6. Repeat the play for the second box.
7. Toss your puck into the top box on the right-hand side.
8. Hop into that box from outside the pattern. Kick the puck into the fourth box and then out of the pattern.
9. Repeat the play for the third box two more times.

10. Toss the puck into the fourth box. Hop into that box and kick the puck out of the pattern.
11. Repeat the play for the fourth box three more times.

PATTERN 3:

6. Toss your puck into the top box on the left-hand side. Hop over the first two boxes into that box. Kick the puck into each box following the arrow directions.
7. Continue tossing your puck into each box in turn. Always jump from the same spot right below the first left-hand box.

Italy

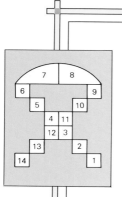

Campana The word *peninsula* means "almost an island." This is a very accurate description of Italy, the European country shaped like a boot and surrounded by the Mediterranean Sea. The sunny, mild climate of Italy allows children to play hopscotch outdoors for many months of the year. The puck is usually a stone or a bottle cap. The word *campana* means "bell."

DIRECTIONS:

1. Throw the puck into box 1.

2. Hop over box 1 into box 2.

3. Jump into boxes 12 and 3, with one foot in each, and jump again into boxes 4 and 11.

4. Continue to hop on the same foot to box 14, following the numbers. Hop back to box 2, and pick up the puck from box 1 as you balance on one foot. Then hop out of the pattern.

5. Repeat steps 1 through 4 with all of the boxes. Treat the double boxes the way you did in Pele, Peregrina, Paradies Hüpfen, and Scotch-Hoppers. The first player to complete the entire pattern wins.

6. You lose a turn if your puck does not land in the correct box, if it touches a line, if you touch a line while hopping, or if your non-hopping foot touches the ground.

Nigeria

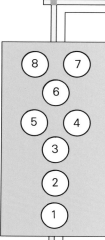

Ta Galagala

If you ask girls in Nigeria if they know a hopping game played in a pattern drawn on the ground, they will answer "Ta Galagala." The name has no meaning in their Hausa language, but adults say the game is "what keeps the children from going to the farm." What they mean is that children sometimes play the game when they should be doing their chores. The pattern consists of eight circular depressions traced in the sandy soil. Nothing is written inside the circles. Each depression is called a *kurtu*. For a puck, girls use a stick or stone called a *kwalo*. If you toss your *kwalo* and it doesn't land inside a *kurtu*, someone will put it in for you, and you can take your turn anyway.

DIRECTIONS:
1. Throw the *kwalo* into circle 1.
2. Hop over circle 1 into circle 2 and then into circle 3. Jump into circles 4 and 5, with one foot in each. Hop into circle 6 and then jump into circles 7 and 8.
3. After you have jumped into circles 7 and 8, clap your hands and jump around to face the other way.
4. Hop back the same way, hopping over circle 1 and turning around to pick up the puck.
5. Throw the puck into each succeeding circle in the same way. Never hop into the circle where the puck lands. Hop over the puck before picking it up on the way back to circle 1.
6. After you have thrown the puck into circle 8 and hopped back to the beginning, throw your puck to a spot just above the pattern (* in the drawing). Proceed to the end of the pattern in the usual way. When you reach 7 and 8, clap your hands and leap around. Bend down and pick up the puck through your legs. Hop back to circle 1 and out of the pattern.
8. If you hop outside a circle or step on a line, or if your puck misses the right circle, then you lose your turn.

People's Republic of China

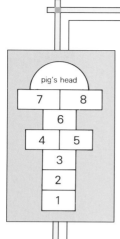

Gat Fei Gei

This game, which originated in China, is also played by children in Chinese communities from New York to San Francisco. The pattern looks somewhat like an airplane. *Gat fei gei* means "one foot jumping flying machine," or "airplane." Many of the homes in China have tile roofs, so children there use a piece of tile as a puck. Children playing the same game in the United States may use a key chain. Sometimes the chain is hooked together to form a circle; at other times it is left unhooked to form a snakelike shape when it lands.

DIRECTIONS:

1. Hop through the eight numbered boxes in sequence and back to box 1. Then hop out.

2. Stand with your toes at the edge of box 1, and toss the puck into the pig's head.

3. Hop through the pattern, landing with two feet in boxes 4 and 5 and 7 and 8. Jump and turn to land again in 7 and 8, this time facing the rest of the pattern, with the pig's head behind you. Now pick up your puck from the pig's head and hop out of the pattern. (Decide before you start the game if players must pick up their pucks by reaching down behind them or by reaching through their legs as they bend forward.) If your hand accidentally touches the ground outside the pig's head, you lose your turn. If you complete this task, you can claim box 1 as your own.

4. The next player follows in the same way.

5. Each player tries to claim boxes until all of the numbered squares are "owned."

6. You may not hop into boxes that are "owned" unless the "owner" has been very generous and marked off a corner, or path, for you to use. You may do the same for other players.

7. When you reach a box that you "own," you must jump in on both feet. If you hop into your box, it is considered "burned," and it becomes available for someone else to "own."

8. After all boxes are "owned," the pig's head can be divided into four parts. You can then compete for those parts just as you did for the body of the airplane.

Poland

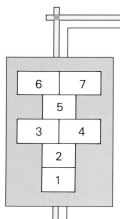

Klassa

Girls in Poland have more than one way to play Klassa, but they always imagine they are hopping into and out of grades (*klassa*) in school. In Breslau (now Wrocław) just after World War II, they used stones to draw the patterns on cement courtyards surrounded by their apartment buildings. Sometimes they used chestnuts as pucks. But the best pucks were the flat pieces of stone that could be found in the piles of rubble left behind from the bombings. There are two ways to play Klassa. One involves only jumping; the other involves both hopping and jumping.

DIRECTIONS:
1. Toss your puck into box 1.

GAME 1:
2. Jump with both feet into box 1 and pick up your puck.
3. Jump into boxes 2 through 7 in sequence and back out again.
4. Toss your puck into box 2. Jump into box 1 and then into box 2 and pick up the puck. Jump all the way through the pattern and back again.
5. Toss the puck into each box in order, and jump through the pattern as you did for the first and second boxes.

6. The first player to make it through the complete pattern without touching a line or misthrowing the puck wins.

GAME 2:
2. Hop on one foot into the box and pick up the puck.
3. Hop into box 2. Jump into boxes 3 and 4, putting one foot in each box. Hop into box 5 and jump into boxes 6 and 7. Jump up and make a turn to land again in boxes 6 and 7.
4. Play the rest of the game as you did in game 1.

Trinidad

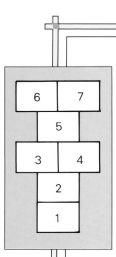

Jumby

Jumby, a word used by English-speaking people of the Caribbean islands, means "spirit" or "ghost." Another word for *jumby* is *duppy*. On the island of Trinidad in the West Indies, over one-third of the people are of black African ancestry. Perhaps they brought the word *jumby* with them when they came from Africa to this island. Any flat surface—dirt or pavement—can provide the space to draw the pattern. The pattern is drawn on pavement with chalk or a soft stone. Children use stones, beanbags, or *jumby beads* (seeds of wild grain beaded with thread) as pucks.

DIRECTIONS:
1. Throw the puck into box 1.
2. Hop over box 1 to land in box 2.
3. Jump to boxes 3 and 4, landing with one foot in each square.
4. Hop to box 5.
5. Jump to boxes 6 and 7, landing with one foot in each square.
6. Jump while turning to land again in boxes 6 and 7, now facing the beginning of the pattern.
7. Hop back to box 5. Jump to boxes 3 and 4, landing with one foot in each box. Hop to box 2.
8. Pick up your puck from box 1.
9. Hop to box 1 and jump out of the pattern.
10. Throw the puck into box 2 and repeat all the steps. Always hop over the box where the puck lands.
11. The first player to get through the entire pattern without a mistake wins.

37

Union of Soviet Socialist Republics

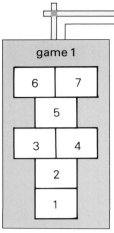

game 1

6	7
	5
3	4
	2
	1

game 2

5	6
4	7
3	8
2	9
1	10

ten classes

5	6
4	7
3	8
2	9
1	10

first exam

Klassiki Moldavia is a republic in the U.S.S.R. In Moldavia, as in Poland, children playing hopscotch imagine they are hopping through the grades in school. The puck is kicked into each box instead of being picked up. The children draw the pattern with chalk on the school-yard asphalt. If they are playing at home, they may draw the pattern with a stick in the dirt in the backyard. The first version of the game was played by an earlier generation of children. The puck was a shoe-polish box weighted with dirt. It was carefully made so that almost everyone, after some practice, would be able to get the puck to land dead center in each box of the pattern. The second version of the game is the way Klassiki is being played in school yards in Moldavia today.

DIRECTIONS:

GAME 1:

1. Toss the puck into box 1.

2. Hop into box 1 and kick the puck with your hopping foot into boxes 2, 3, 4, 5, 6, and 7 as you hop into each square. Kick it back the same way—into each box as you hop—all the way to box 1 and out of the pattern.

3. Toss the puck into box 2. Hop over box 1 and land in box 2. Kick the puck into box 3 and so on through the pattern.

4. Toss the puck into box 3 and hop over boxes 1 and 2 into box 3. Kick the puck into each of the boxes just as you did before.

5. Toss the puck into box 4. Hop into box 4 and continue to play as above.

6. When you toss the puck into boxes 5, 6, and 7, you can jump into boxes 3 and 4 on both feet before hopping into boxes 5, 6, and 7.

GAME 2:

1. Toss the puck into box 1. Hop into box 1. With your hopping foot, kick the puck into box 2, then 3, and all the way to box 10 and out of the pattern.

2. Toss the puck into box 2. Hop into box 1. Hop into box 2, and kick the puck into box 3, then 4, and all the way to 10 and out as you did earlier.

3. Keep going in the same way until you have tossed the puck into box 10.

4. To win the game, you must pass ten classes and two exams. For the first exam, toss the puck into box 1. Hop into box 1, and kick the puck into the boxes in the order shown in the drawings: 9, 3, 7, 5, 6, 4, 8, 2, 10, and out (as you follow the puck).

5. For the second exam, toss the puck into box 1. Hop into box 1 and kick the puck into box 3. Hop into box 2, then into box 3, and kick the puck into box 5. Hop into box 4, then 5, and kick the puck into box 6.

6. Continue down this side of the pattern, skipping one class (or box) as you did before, all the way to box 10 and out of the pattern.

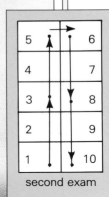

second exam

39

18235

United States

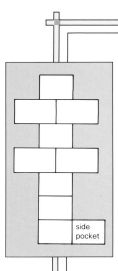

side
pocket

Alaskan Hopscotch

Summer in Alaska is not exactly like summer anywhere in the forty-eight states south of it. The days are very long, sometimes with only a few hours of darkness. Although it can be colder in Unalakleet, Alaska, in summer than it is in Texas in the winter, it is still warm enough to play outside. The land is green and, in early summer, covered with wild flowers. The warm days are welcome after winter temperatures that may be as low as fifty degrees below zero. Hopscotch as played by the Alaskans is similar to other hopscotch games. The puck, usually a rock, is called a *man* and is large and square (about two inches high and two inches wide). The boxes are neither named nor numbered.

DIRECTIONS:

1. Decide whether or not you will allow a "side pocket." This is shown on the pattern as a box beside the first box. The side pocket makes the toss more challenging or gives you a running start when you start jumping through the pattern.

2. Decide which foot you will hop on—your right or your left. You cannot touch a line or hop into a box with a puck in it.

3. Everyone playing tosses his or her puck into the box nearest the side pocket. The first player then takes his or her turn.

4. Hop over the first box, through the remaining boxes, and back to the box above or next to where all the players' men are. Pick up your man and hop out of the pattern. Then throw your man into the next highest box. Follow the usual rules for double boxes.

5. The next player repeats the steps except that he or she must not hop into the box with the first player's man. The side pocket can be used to make a diagonal leap into a hard-to-reach box. You *cannot* enter the first box with anything but a hop.

6. Players take turns moving their men and hopping through the pattern.

7. If you toss your man and it doesn't land in the box, you lose a turn.

8. After you have moved your man through all of the numbers, you must complete one more turn through the pattern reciting the letters of the alphabet as you hop.

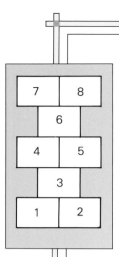

Potsy

Girls who are now grandmothers or even great-grandmothers played Potsy in Brooklyn, and in all the other boroughs of New York, the same way it is played today. Brooklyn has cement sidewalks and blacktop streets, so the Potsy pattern can be drawn just about anywhere. Usually this hopscotch game is played by girls, and the pattern is drawn with chalk or a rock. The puck is also called a *potsy* and can be almost anything: safety pins clipped together, a stone, keys on a chain, or a broken piece of china. Potsy is played whenever it is neither too hot nor too cold.

DIRECTIONS:
1. Toss the potsy into box 1.
2. Hop into box 2.
3. Hop into box 3, then jump into boxes 4 and 5, with one foot in each box. Hop into box 6, and then jump into boxes 7 and 8.
4. Jump up and turn around, landing again in boxes 7 and 8, this time facing the pattern.
5. Hop and jump back to box 2. Lean down and pick up the potsy from box 1. Hop out of the pattern.
6. Throw the potsy into each succeeding box. Never hop into the box with the potsy in it.
7. If you complete the whole pattern without any mistakes, you can choose a box and put your initials in it. The next players cannot jump into your initialed box.

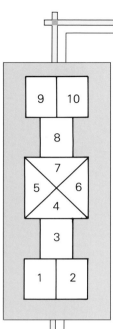

Texan Hopscotch

During my childhood in the north Texas town of Denton, children chalked hopscotch patterns on sidewalks shaded by large mulberry trees. When the mulberries fell from the trees, they made purplish polka dots in the hopscotch patterns. Nearby grocery stores sold bottled soft drinks from boxes filled with water and ice. The front of the box had another box attached to it that held bottle caps. These caps were often used as pucks in games of hopscotch. The rubber heel from a shoe or a flat rock was also used.

DIRECTIONS:

1. Throw the puck into box 1.

2. Jump into boxes 1 and 2, with one foot in each box.

3. Hop into box 3 and then into box 4. Jump into boxes 5 and 6, with one foot in each box.

4. Hop into box 7 and box 8. Jump into boxes 9 and 10, with one foot in each box.

5. Jump up and turn to face the beginning of the pattern, landing with your feet still in boxes 9 and 10. Continue to hop and jump back to the box where your puck is. Pick it up and hop out of the pattern.

6. Throw your puck into each box in sequence, and hop through the pattern in the same way.

7. You lose your turn if you hop on a line or if your puck misses the box you aimed for or lands on a line.

8. The first player to complete all ten throws wins the game.

Bibliography

Research on the subject of hopscotch has led me from library to library through the vast resources of the interlibrary loan system. Frequently, I would find only a small paragraph about hopscotch, but many times a book would include detailed drawings of variations of the game. Although Frederick V. Grunfield in *Games of the World* (Holt, Rinehart and Winston, 1975) cites catalogued research of nearly twenty versions of hopscotch played in the streets and playgrounds of San Francisco and states that "whole books have been written about the hopscotch varieties to be found in the cities," we were unable to locate many of these titles.

Persistence did lead to some wonderful finds, however; and the detective work of research has been fascinating. As an example, through Ron Jobe of the University of British Columbia, Department of Education, I learned of a book called *Hopscotch*, written by Patricia Evans and published by the Porpoise Bookshop in 1955. Beverly Braun, Director of Library-Instructional Services at Hartnell College, Salinas, California, then helped me find the complete citation in Hartnell's computer data base. Finally, through interlibrary loan, I was able to borrow this small paperback from the New Orleans Public Library.

The following books were most helpful in completing the research and selecting the games we have included in this book:

Bancroft, Jesse H. *Games*, revised and enlarged ed. of *Games for the Playground, Home, School, and Gymnasium*. New York: Macmillan, 1937. Detailed versions of hopscotch include United States, Italian, French (Marraine), English (Hop-and-Jump), Snail Hop Scotch, and Monte Carlo.

Brewster, Paul G. *American Nonsinging Games*. Norman: University of Oklahoma Press, 1953. Variations of hopscotch found in the United States include Tennessee, Missouri, New York, Iowa, Indiana, and Oklahoma.

Champlin, John D., and Arthur E. Bostwick. *The Young Folks' Cyclopaedia of Games and Sports*. New York: Henry Holt, 1890. Brief historical sketches and descriptions of foreign varieties of games.

Evans, Patricia. *Hopscotch*. San Francisco: The Porpoise Bookshop, 1955. History and game variations collected in San Francisco in 1955.

Ferretti, Fred. *The Great American Book of Sidewalk, Stoop, Dirt, Curb, and Alley Games*. New York: Workman Publishing Company, 1975. Describes variations of American hopscotch names: Boston, Hopscotch; Chicago, Sky Blue; Far West, Potsie, Pottsie, Pottsy, or Potsy. Also Italian, Austrian, and Chinese variations. Describes pattern or playing court, rules, and variations.

Gallagher, Rachel. *Games in the Street*. New York: Four Winds Press, 1976. Explains the name variations: Spain, La Escalera de Caracol; Sri Lanka, Masop or Tatto; Philippines, Picko or Buan-Buan; Hawaii, Ki-no-a.

Geri, Frank H. *Illustrated Games, Rhythms, and Stunts for Children*. Englewood Cliffs, N.J.: Prentice-Hall, 1957. Describes Home Hopscotch or Snail.

Gomme, Alice Bertha. *The Traditional Games of England, Scotland, and Ireland*. Oxford, England: Thames and Hudson, 1984. Eight hundred titles of games for children collected in England, Ireland, and Scotland. Shows ten patterns, with history.

Grunfield, Frederic, ed. *Games of the World, How to Make Them, How to Play Them, How They Came to Be*. New York: Holt, Rinehart and Winston, 1975. Six games are described with the Dutch rules: Heaven and Earth Hopscotch, Water Hopscotch, Send-a-Letter Hopscotch, Monday-Tuesday Hopscotch, English Hopscotch, Moon Hopscotch.

Ichper Book of Worldwide Games and Dances. Washington, D.C.: International Council on Health, Physical Education, and Recreation, 1967. Provides patterns and rules for games from Bolivia (La Thunkuña), Great Britain (Hop Scotch and Round Hopscotch), Germany (Hinkspiel), and Yugoslavia (Na Kolo).

Johnson, June. *The Outdoor-Indoor Fun Book*. New York: Harper, 1961. Patterns for five versions: Basic Forms, Square Hopscotch, Beanbag Hop, Ishigetigoko, and Spiral Hop.

Milberg, Alan. *Street Games*. New York: McGraw-Hill, 1976. Discusses origin, general rules, and details of Italian hopscotch (Sky Blue), six variations of French hopscotch (*marelle*), English Hopscotch, and Snail Hopscotch.

Mulac, Margaret E. *Games and Stunts for Schools, Camps, and Playgrounds*. New York: Harper & Row, 1964. Outlines Category Hopscotch, English Hopscotch, French Hopscotch, Italian Hopscotch, Jumpscotch, Pitch and Capture, Sidewalk London, and Snail Hopscotch.

Newell, William Wells. *Games and Songs of American Children*. New York: Dover Publications, 1963. Pattern for one United States version.

Opie, Iona, and Peter Opie. *Children's Games in Street and Playground*. Oxford, England: Clarendon Press, 1969. Briefly describes problems in drawing diagrams for hopscotch.

Sandoval, Ruben. *Games, Games, Games, Juegos, Juegos, Juegos, Chicano Children at Play—Games and Rhymes*. New York: Doubleday, 1977. Describes the Snail (el Caracol), and names variations (Drink Milk [Bebe Leche], Big [Grande], and the Horse [el Caballo]).

Simmons, Anne, Marcella Porter, and Irene Norman. *Child's Play, Vigorous Activities with a Limited Budget*. Springfield, Ill.: Charles C. Thomas, 1982. Includes basic hopscotch play, Diamond Hopscotch, Follow the Leader Hopscotch, and Trapezoid Hopscotch.

Sutton-Smith, Brian. *The Folkgames of Children*. Austin: University of Texas Press, 1972. Historical background of New Zealand Hopscotch with variations: Rectangular Hopscotch or Kick the Block, Avenue Hopscotch, Donkey, Round-the-World Hopping, Snake, Snail, and Maze.

Vinton, Iris. *The Folkways Omnibus of Children's Games*. New York: Stackpole Books, 1970. Describes "games played on the Great North Road, built by the Romans in Britain."

Wiswell, Phil. *Kids' Games: Traditional Indoor and Outdoor Activities for Children of All Ages*. New York: Doubleday, 1987. Three basic outlines with optional rules.

Yerian, Cameron, and Margaret Yerian, eds. *Fun-Time Games for One, Two, or More*. Chicago: Children's Press, 1974. Describes hopscotch as played in Norway, Burma, and Vietnam.

Index